THE

GRAND GRIMOIRE

THE

GRAND GRIMOIRE

or the art of controlling celestial, aerial, terrestrial, and infernal spirits.

With the TRUE SECRET of speaking with the dead, winning whenever playing the lottery, discovering hidden treasure, etc.

Printed from a manuscript of 1522.

THE FIRST BOOK

CHAPTER I

So rare is this great work, so much has it been sought after in these parts, that by reason of its scarcity, one may well call it, with the Rabbinical authors, the veritable *Magnum Opus*; it is they who have bequeathed to us this priceless original, which innumerable charlatans have impotently endeavoured to counterfeit, in imitation of the genuine book, which they have never succeeded in discovering, and for the appropriation of the money of simpletons who have recourse to the first that offers himself instead of to the fountain-head.

The present copy has been transcribed from the genuine writings of the mighty King Solomon, which have been met with by pure chance, this sublime monarch having passed all the days of his life in he most laborious researches and in pursuit of the most obscure and hopeless secrets; but in the end he succeeded in all his undertakings, penetrating even into the most remote haunts of Spirits, whom he bound one and all, and forced them to obey him by the power of his *Talisman* or *Clavicle*. Of a truth, what other man, save this invincible genius, would have had the hardihood to reveal the withering words which God makes use of to strike terror into the rebellious Angels and to compel them into obedience?

Having soared into the celestial altitudes that he might master the secrets and learn the omnipotent words which constitute all the

9

power of a terrible and venerable Deity, the essence of whose innermost arcana, made use of by an infinite Divinity, was extracted by this grand King, and thereby he has discovered us the Stellar Influences, the constellation of the planets, and the method. for the Evocation of all hierarchies of Spirits, by the recitation of the sublime Apellations as they are hereafter set down for you in this Book, as well as the true composition and effects of the dreadful Blasting Rod which causes the Spirits to tremble, and which God also used to arm His Angel when Adam and Eve were driven out of the Terrestrial Paradise, and wherewith he smote the rebellious Angels, precipitating their ambitions into the most appalling gulfs by the power of this very Rod- this Rod which collects the clouds, which disperses and breaks up tempests, storms, thunderbolts, and precipitates them upon any portion of the Earth at the pleasure of its director.

Now, therefore, hereinafter follow the true words which have comeforth from his mouth, which I have literally followed, and in which I have experienced all possible delight, doubt, and satisfaction, since I have bad the good fortune to succeed in all my undertakings.

ANTONIO VENITIANA *del Rabina.*

CHAPTER II

Oh, men! oh, impotent mortals I tremble at your own temerity when you blindly aspire to the possession of a science so profound. Lift up your minds beyond your limited sphere, and learn of me that before you undertake anything, it is necessary that you should become firm and immoveable, besides being scrupulously attentive in the exact observation, step by step, of all things whatsoever I shall tell you, without which precautions every operation will turn to your disadvantage, confusion, and total destruction; while, on the contrary, by following my injunctions with precision, you will rise from your meanness and poverty, achieving a complete success in all your enterprises.

Arm yourselves, therefore, with intrepidity, prudence, wisdom, and virtue, as qualifications for this grand and illimitable Work, in which I have passed sixty and seven years, working night and day for the attainment of success in this sublime object. The faithful performance of all that is hereinafter set down is the indispensable condition of achievement.

You must abstain during an entire quarter of the Moon from the society of females, so as to protect yourself from the possibility of impurity. You must commence your magical quarter at the same moment with that of the luminary itself, by a pledge to the Grand Adonay, who is the master of all Spirits, to make no more than two collections daily, that is to say, in every twenty-four hours of the said quarter of the Moon, which collations should be taken at noon and midnight, or, if it better please you, at seven o'clock in the morning and at the corresponding hour in the evening, using the following prayer previously to each repast during the whole of the said quarter.

PRAYER

I implore thee, oh, thou grand and powerful *Adonay*, Master of all Spirits, I beseech thee, o Eloim, I implore thee, o Jehovam! o grand Adonay, I give thee my soul, my heart, my bowels, my hands, my feet, my desires, my entire being! o grand Adonay, deign to be favourable unto me! So be it! Amen.

Then take your repast; disrobe as seldom and sleep as little possible during the whole of the said period, but meditate continually on your undertaking, centering all your hopes in the infinite goodness of the great *Adonay*. Afterwards, on the morning which succeeds the first night of the said quarter of the Moon, go to a druggist's and purchase a blood-stone called *Ematille*, which must be carried contintially about you for fear of accident, and in expectation that henceforth the Spirit whom you propose to compel and to bind will do all in his power to overwhelm you with terror so as to incite you to abandon your enterprise, hoping in this manner to escape from the evils which you are beginning to weave about him. It must be carefully borne in mind that there should be either one or three taking part in the evocation, the *Karcist* included, who is the person appointed to address the Spirit, holding the Destroying Rod in his hand. Be careful to select as the scene of the evocation a forlorn and isolated spot, where the *Karcist* will be free from interruption. You must then purchase a virgin kid, and decapitate it on the third day of the Moon, with a garland of vervain wound about the neck, immediately below the head, by means of a green ribbon. Transport the animal to the place chosen for the evocation, and there, with the right arm bared to the shoulder, arming yourself with a blade of pure steel, and having kindled a fire of white wood, recite the following word, in a hopeful and animated manner:

INITIAL OFFERING

I immolate this victim to thee, oh ! grant Adonay, Eloim, Ariel, and Jehovam, to the honour, glory, and power of thy nature which is superior to all Spirits. O grand Adonay! vouchsafe to receive it as an acceptable offering. Amen

Here you must cut the throat of the Kid, skin it, set the body on the fire, and reduce it to ashes, which must be collected and cast towards the Rising of the Sun, at the same time repeating the following words:

It is to the honour, glory, and dominion of thy name, oh grand Adonay, Eloim, Ariel, and Jehovam, that I spill the blood of this victim! Vouchsafe, o thou grand Adonay, to receive its ashs as an acceptable sacrifice!

While the victim is being consumed by the flames, you may rejoice in the honour and glory of the grand Adonay, Eloim, Ariel, and Jehovam, taking care to preserve the skin of the virgin Kid to form the round or Grand Kabbalistic Circle which you must place yourself on the day of the grand enterprise.

CHAPTER III

CONTAINS THE TRUE COMTOSITION OF THE MYSTERIOUS WAND OR DESTROYING ROD.

On the eve of the grand Enterprise, you must go in search of a Wand or Rod of wild hazel which has never borne fruit; its length should be nineteen inches and a half. When you have met with a Wand of the required form, touch it not otherwise than with your eyes; let it stay till the next morning, which is the day of action; then must you cut it absolutely at the moment when the Sun rises; strip it of its leaves and minor branches if any there be, using the same steel blade with which the victim was slain, which will still be stained with its blood, assuming that you have abstained from wiping it. Begin to cut it when the sun is first rising over this hemisphere, pronouncing the following words:

I beseech Thee, O grand Adonay, Eloim, Ariel, and Jehovam to be propitious unto me, and to endow this Wand which I am cutting with the power and virtue of those of Jacob, of Moses, and of the mighty Josua!

I also beseech Thee, O grand Adonay, Eloim, Ariel, and Jehovam to infuse into this Rod the whole strength of Samson, the righteous wrath of Emanuel, and the thunders of powerful *Zariatnatmik*, who will avenge the crime of men at the great day of judgment! Amen.

Having pronounced these sublime and terrific words, and still keeping the eye turned to the quarter of the Rising Sun, you may finish cutting your Rod, and may then carry it to your room. You must then go in search of a piece of wood, which you must fashion to the same size as the two ends of the genuine Rod, and take it to an ironmaster to weld the two little branches with the steel blade with which the victim was slain, taking care that the ends are slightly pointed when they are fitted to the wood; the whole being executed after this manner, you may return home and fix the before-mentioned with your own hands to the genuine Rod. Subsequently you must use a piece of loadstone to maguetise the two points, pronouncing the following words:

By the grand Adonay, Eloim, Anal, and Jehhoam, I bid thee be united to and attract all substances which I desire by the might of the sublime Adonay, Eloim, Ariel, and Jehovam. I command thee by the opposition of fire and water to separate all substances as they were separated on the day of the world's creation. Amen.

Finally, you must rejoice in the honour and glory of the sublime Adonay, being convinced that you are in possession of a most priceless treasure of the light. On the following evening collect your Rod, goatskin, the stone called Ematille, and the two Vervain crowns, as well as two candlesticks and two candles of virgin wax, made by a virgin girl and duly blessed. Take also a new steel, two new flints with sufficient tinder to kindle a fire, likewise half a bottle of brandy, some blessed incense and camphor, and four nails from the coffin of a dead child. All these must be carried to the place chosen for the great work, where everything hereinafter laid down must be scrupulously performed and the dread Kabbalistic Circle must be described in an accurate manner.

TRIANGOLO

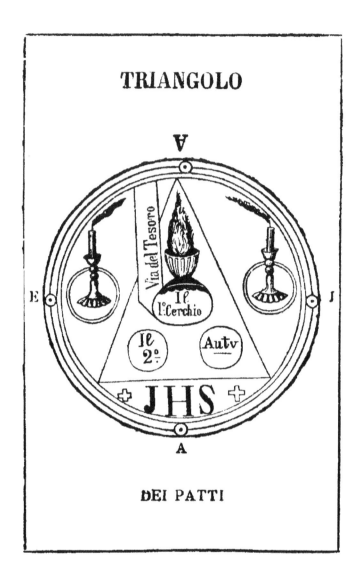

DEI PATTI

CHAPTER IV

CONTAINING A TRUE REPRESENTATION OF THE GRAND KABBALISTIC CIRCLE.

You must begin by forming a Circle with strips of Kid's skin, fastened to the ground by means of your four nails. Then with the stone called Ematille you must trace the triangle within the Circle beginning at the Eastern point. A large A, a small E, a small A, and a small J, must be drawn in like manner, as also the sacred name of Jesus between two Crosses. By this means the spirits will have no power to harm you from behind. The Karcist and his assistants may then fearlessly proceed to their places within the triangle, and regardless of any noises may set the two candlesticks and the two vervain crowns on the right and left sides of the Triangle within the Circle. This being done, you may light your two candles, taking care that there is a new brazier in front of the Karcist, piled with newly consecrated charcoal. This must be kindled by the Karcist casting a small quantity of the Brandy therein and a part of the camphor, the rest being reserved to feed the fire periodically, in proportion to the length of the business. Having punctually performed all that is mentioned above, you may repeat the following prayer:

I present thee, O great Adonay! this incense as the purest I can obtain; in like manner, I present thee this charcoal prepared from the most ethereal of woods. I offer them, O grand and omnipotent Adonay, Eloim, Ariel, and Jehovam, with my whole soul and my whole heart. Vouchsafe, O great Adonay! to receive them as an acceptable holocaust. Amen.

You should also be careful to have no alloyed metal about your person, except a gold or silver coin, wrapped in paper, which you must fling to the spirit when he appears outside the circle, so as to prevent him from harming you. While he is picking up the coin, begin promptly the following prayer, fortifying yourself with courage, energy, and prudence. Be, also, especially careful that the Karcist is he sole speaker; the assistants must preserve a determined silence, even if they are questioned or menaced by the Spirit.

FIRST PRAYER

O great and living God, subsisting in one and the same person, the Father, the Son, and the Holy Ghost, I adore Thee with the deepest veneration, and I submit with the liveliest confidence to Thy holy and sufficient protection; I believe with the most sincere faith that Thou art my Creator, my Benefactor, my Preserver, and my Lord, and I testify to thy sovereign Majesty that my soul desire is to belong to Thee through the whole of eternity. So be it! Amen.

SECOND PRAYER

O great and living God, who hast created man to enjoy felicity in this life, who hast adapted all things for his necessities, and who didst declare that everything should be made subject to his will, be favourable to this my design, and permit not the rebellious spirits to be in possession of those treasures which were formed by Thine own hands for our temporal requirements. Grant me, O great God, the power to dispose of them by the potent and terrific names in Thy Clavicle: Adonay, Eloim, Ariel, Jehovam, Tagla, Mathon, be ye propitious unto
me. So be it! Amen.

Be careful to nourish the flame with brandy, incense, and camphor, and proceed with the offertory by means of the following prayer.

OFFERTORY

I offer Thee this incense as the purest which I have been able to obtain, O sublime Adonay, Eloim, Ariel, and Jehovam! vouchsafe to receive it as an acceptable holocaust. Incline to me in Thy power, and enable me to succeed in this great enterprise. So be it. Amen.

FIRST CONJURATION

ADDRESSED TO THE EMPEROR LUCIFER.

Emperor Lucifer, Master and Prince of Rebellious Spirits, I adjure thee to leave thine abode in whatsoever quarter of the world it may be situated, and come hither to communicate with me. I command and I conjure thee in the name of the mighty living God: Father, Son, and Holy Ghost: to appear without noise and without any evil smell, to respond in a clear and intelligible voice, point by point, to all that I shall ask thee, failing which, thou shalt be most surely compelled to obedience by the power of the divine Adonay, Eloim, Ariel, Jehovam, Tagla, Mathon, and by the whole hierarchy of superior Intelligences, who shall constrain thee against thy will. *Venite, Venite!*

Submiritillor LUCIFUGE, or eternal torment shall overwhelm thee, by the great power of this Blasting Rod. *In Subito.*

SECOND CONJURATION

I command and I adjure thee, Emperor Lucifer, as the representative of the mighty living God, and by the power of Emanuel his only son, who is thy master and mine, and by the virtue of His precious blood, which he shed to redeem mankind from thy chains, I command thee to quit thine abode wheresoever it may be, swearing that I will give thee one quarter of one bour of quiet alone, if thou dost not straightway come hither and communicate with me in an audible and intelligible voice, or if thy personal presence be impossible to send me thy Messenger Astarot in a human form, without either noise or evil smell, failing which I will smite thee and thy whole race with the terrible Blasting Rod into the depth of the bottomless abysses, and that by the power of those great words in the Clavicle- *By Adonay, Eloim, Ariel, Jehovam, Tagla, Mathon, Almouzin, Arios, Pithona, Magots, Sylphae, Tabots, Salamandrae, Guonus, Terrae, Caelis, Godens, Aqua.* In subito.

NOTICE.- Before uttering the third Conjuration, should the Spirit refuse to comply, read what follows in the Clavicle, and smite all the Spirits, by plunging both the forked extremities of your Rod into the flames, and be not alarmed, in so doing, at tbe frightful howls which you may hear, for at this extreme moment all the Spirits will manifest. Then, before reading the Clavicle, and in the midst of the commotion, recite the third conjuration.

THIRD CONJURATION

I adjure thee, Emperor Lucifer, as the agent of the strong living God, of His beloved Son, and of the Holy Ghost, and by the power of the great Adonay, Eloim, Ariel, and Jehovam, to appear instantly, or to send me thy Messenger Astarot, forcing thee to forsake thy hiding place, wheresoever it may be, and warning thee that if thou dost not manifest this moment, I will straightway smite thee and all thy race with the Blasting Rod of the great Adonay, Eloim, Ariel, and Jehovam, etc.

At this point, should the Spirit still fail to appear, plunge the two ends of your Rod a second time into the flames, and recite the following potent words from the grand Clavicle of Solomon.

GRAND CONJURATION

EXTRACTED FROM THE VERITABLE CLAVICLE.

I adiure thee, O Spirit by the power of the Grand Adonay, to appear instanter, and by Eloim, by Ariel, by Jehovam, by Aqua, Tagla, Mathon, Oarios, Almoazin, Arios, Membrot, Varios, Pithona, Majods, Salphae, Gabots, Salamandrae, Tabots, Gnomus, Terrae, Coelis, Godens, Aqua, Gingua, Janna, Etitnamus, Zariatnatmix, etc.

A..E..A..J..A..T..M..
O..A..A..M..V..P..M..S..C..S..T..G..T..C..G..A..G..J...F...Z...etc.

After a second repetition of these sublime and powerful words, you may be sure that the Spirit will respond after the ensuing manner.

Of the manifestation of the Spirit

Lo, I am here! What dost thou seek of me? Why dost thou disturb my repose? Smite me no more with that dread Rod!

--LUCIFUGE' ROFOCALE.

LUCIFUGE' ROFOCALE

LUCIFUGE' ROFOCALE

Reply to the Spirit.

30

Hadst thou appeared when I invoked thee, I had by no means smitten thee; remember if the request which I make thee be refused, I am determined to torment thee eternally.

--SOLOMON.

The Spirit's Answer.

Torment me no further. Say, rather, what thou dost require at my hands.

--LUCIFUGE' ROFOCALE.

The Requisition.

I require that thou shalt communicate two several times on each night of the week either with myself or with those who are entrusted with my present Book, the which thou shalt approve and sign; I permit thee the choice of those hours which may suit thee, if thou approvest not those which I now enumerate.

To Wit:

On Monday at Nine o'clock and at midnight.
On Tuesday at Ten o'clock and at One in the morning.
On Wednesday at Eleven o'clock and at Two in the morning.
On Thursday at Eight and Ten o'clock.
On Friday at Seven in the evening and at mid night.
On Saturday at Nine in the evening and a Eleven at night.

Further, I command thee to surrender me the nearest Treasure, and I promise thee as a reward the first piece of gold or silver which I lay hands on on the first day of every month. Such is my demand.

--SOLOMON.

The Spirit's Reply.

I cannot comply with thy request on such terms nor on any others, unless thou shalt give thyself over to me in fifty years, to do with thy body and soul as I please.

--LUCIFUGE' ROFOCALE.

Rejoinder to the Spirit.

Lo, will I smite thee and thy whole race, by the might of great Adonay, if, on the contrary, thou dost not comply with my request.

NOTICE.
You plunge the points of the Blasting Rod into the fire and repeat the grand Conjuration of the Clavicle, till the Spirit surrenders himself to your will.

Answer and Compliance of the Spirit.

Smite me no further; I pledge myself to do what thou desirest two several times on every night of the week.

To wit:

> On Monday at Ten o'clock and at midnight.
> On Tuesday at Eleven o'clock and at One ii the morning.
> On Wednesday at midnight and at Two in th morning.
> On Thursday at Eight and Eleven o'clock.
> On Friday at Nine o'clock and at midnight.
> On Saturday at Ten o'clock and at One in the morning.

I also approve thy Book, and I give thee my true Signature on Parchment, which thou shalt affix at its end, to make use of at thy need. Further, I place myself at thy disposition, to appear before thee at thy call when, being purified, an holding the dreadful Blasting Rod, thou shalt open the Book, having described the great Kabbalistic Circle, and pronounced the word *Rofocale*. I promise thee to have friendly commerce with those who are fortified by the possession of the said Book, where my true signature stands, provided that they invoke me according to rule, on the first occasion that they require me.

I also engage to deliver thee the treasure which thou seekest, on condition that thou keepest the secret for ever inviolable, art charitable to the Poor, and dost give me a gold or silver coin on the first day of every month. If thou failest, tho art mine everlastingly.

--LUCIFUGE' ROFOCALE.

Imprimatur.

Reply to the Spirit.

I agree to thy conditions.

--SOLOMON.

INVITATION OF THE SPIRIT

FOLLOW ME, AND COME LAY THY BANDS ON THE TREASURE.

Thereupon the Karcist, armed with the Blasting Rod and the stone called Ematille shall issue from the Circle at that point where the door of mighty Adonay is figured, and shall follow the Spirit, but the assistants shall not stir one step from the Circle, but shall remain firm and immoveable within it, whatever reports they hear, and whatever visions they see. The Spirit shall then conduct the Karcist to the vicinity of the Treasure, when it may befall that the Karcist shall behold the apparition of a large and fierce dog with a collar as resplendent as the Sun. This will be a Gnome, which he can drive off by presenting the point of his Rod, when the apparition will make off towards the Treasure. The Karcist must follow, and on reaching the Treasure will be astonished to discover the person who has hidden it, who will endeavour to grapple with him, but will be unable so much as to approach him. The Karcist must be provided with a sheet of virgin parchment inscribed with the grand Conjuration of the Clavicle. This he must cast upon the Treasure grasping one of its coins at the same moment as a pledge and a surety, and previously flinging down a piece of his own money bitten by his own teeth, after which he may retire, walking backwards and carrying away what he can of the Treasure. The rest cannot escape him after the above precautions. He must, however, take heed not to turn round, whatever noise he may hear, for at this critical moment it will truly seem as if all the mountains in the world were being precipitated upon him. He must for this cause be fortified with special intrepidity, must take fright at nothing, and keep perfectly firm. So acting, he will he led back by the Spirit to the entrance of the Circle. Then shall the Karcist recite the following discharge of the Spirit.

CONJURATION

AND DISCHARGE OF THE SPIRIT.

Oh Prince Lucifer, I am, for the time, contented with thee; I now leave thee in peace, and permit thee to retire wheresover it may seem good to thee, so it be without noise and without leaving any evil smell behind thee. Be mindful, however, of our engagement, for should'st thou fail in it, even for a moment, be assured that I shall eternally smite thee with the Blasting Rod of the great Adonay, Eloim, Ariel and Jehovam. Amen.

ACT OF THANKSGIVING

O omnipotent God, who hast created all things for the service and convenience of men, we return Thee most humble thanks for the benefits which, in Thy great bounty, Thou hast poured out on us during this night of Thine inestimable favours, and for that which thou hast granted us according to our desires! Now, O almighty God, have we realized all the scope of thy great promises when Thou didst say to us- seek and ye shall find, knock and it shall he opened unto you. And as Thou hast commanded and Warned us to succour the poor, we promise Thee, in the presence of the great Adonay, Eloim, Ariel, and Jehovam, to be charitable and to pour out on them the beneficient beams of the sun with which those four potent divinities have enriched us! So be it. Amen.

VALE.

THE SECOND BOOK

Containing the genuine Sanctum Regnum of the Clavicle, or the true method of making Pacts. Together with the Names, Offices, and Characters of all the chief Superior Intelligences; so, also, the method to compel their appearance by virtue of the great Conjuration in the chapter entitled "Pacts," which enforces their obedience in any desired Operation.

The genuine SANCTUM REGNUM of the grand Clavicle, otherwise termed the Pacta Conventa Daemoniorum, so long talked about, is a matter eminently calling for explanation in this place, for the information of those who are desirous to bind Spirits, but who are devoid of the requisite resources for composing the Blasting Rod and the Kabbalistic Circle, as described in the foregoing book. Such persons will never succeed in evoking any Spirits unless they perform, point by point, all that is detailed herein after, concerning the manner of making Pacts with any Spirits whatsoever, whether for the possession of Treasures, for the enjoyment of women or girls, and for obtaining any desired favour at their hands, whether for the discovery of the most hidden secrets in all the Courts and Cabinets of the world, whether for the revelation of the most impenetrable mysteries, whether for engaging a Spirit to perform one's work in the night, whether to cause a fall of hail or a storm in any appointed place, whether to open seals, to be-hold what is passing in private houses, and learn all the skill of the Shepherds, whether to obtain the Hand of Glory, and discern all the qualities and virtues of Metals, Minerals, and Vegetables, and of Animals both pure and impure, and to perform things so astounding that no person in existence can fail to be in a condition of utter bewilderment to see that by means of a Pact with certain Spirits, one can discover the grandest secrets of Nature, which are hidden from the eyes of all other men. It is to the Clavicle of the great King Solomon that we owe the discovery of the genuine method of making Pacts, which he also made use of himself for the acquisition of his immense riches, for the pleasure of such innumerable women, and for the revelation of the most impenetrable arcana of nature, whereby every species of good and evil may be accomplished.

We shall begin, in the first place, hy enumerating the names of the Chief Spirits, with their Powers and Dominions, and shall afterwards explain the *Pacta Daemoniorum*, or the true method of making Pacts, with any Spirits whatsoever. Hereinafter follow the names of the principal infernal Spirits.

LUCIFER- Emperor.
BELZEBUTH- Prince.
ASTAROT- Grand Duke.

Then follow tile superior Spirits, who are subordinate to those just named. To wit:

LUCIFUGE'- Prime Minister.
SATANACHIA- Commander-in-Chief.
AGALIAREPT- Another Commander.
FLEURETY- Lieutenant-General.
SARGATANAS- Brigadier-Major.
NEBIROS- Field-Marshal.

The six chief Spirits who are named above have control over the whole Infernal Power which is entrusted to the lesser Spirits. They have eighteen other Intelligences at their disposal, and who are subordinated unto them.

To wit:

1. *Bael.*
2. *Agares.*
3. *Marbas.*
4. *Pruslas.*
5. *Aamon.*
6. *Barbatos.*
7. *Buer.*
8. *Gusoyn.*
9. *Botis.*

10. *Bathim.*
11. *Pursan.*
12. *Eligor.*
13. *Zoray.*
14. *Valefar.*
15. *Faraii.*
16. *Ayperos.*
17. *Naberrs.*
18. *Glassyalabolas.*

TRIANGLE

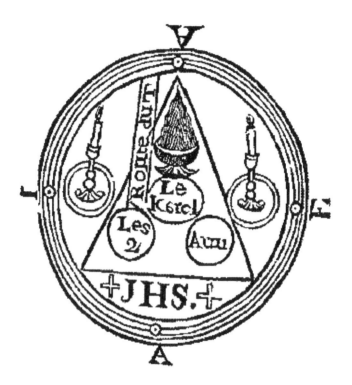

DES PACTES.

Having enumerated the names of these eighteen spirits who are inferior to the previous six, it will be well to acquaint you with the matters which follow.

To wit:

LUCIFUGE' has power over the three first, namely, over *Bael, Agares, and Marbas.*
    SATANACHIA has power over *Pruslas, Aamon, and Barbatos.*
    AGALIAREPT has power over *Buer, Gusoyn, and Botis.*
    FLEURETY has power over *Bathim, Pursan, and Eligor.*
    SARGATANAS has power over *Zoray, Valefar, and Faraii.*
    NEBIROS has power over *Ayperos, Naberrs, and Glassyalebolas.*

And albeit there are millions of other spirits in subordination to those which have been enumerated, it will serve no purpose to name them, as they are only required when it pleases the Superior Spirits to employ them in place of themselves, for they make use of all the inferior Intelligencies, as if they were their workmen or slaves. Thus in making the Pact with any of the six governors of whom you may be in need, it is unimportant what Spirit obeys you. Notwithstanding, invariably require of the Spirit with whom you make your Pact that you shall be served by one of the three superiors among his special subordinates.

Here follow the precise Powers, Attainments, Arts, and Faculties of the above mentioned spirits, so that any one who is eager to make a Pact, can recognise among the qualities, the ones which will serve his need.

The first is the great *Lucefuge' Rofocale*, Prime Minister Infernal; he has the control, with which Lucifer has invested him, over all the wealth and treasures of the world.

The second is the grand SATANACHIA, General in Chief, he has the power of subjecting all women and girls to his wishes, and to do with them as he wills.

AGALIAREPT, another commander, has the faculty of discovering the arcane secrets in all the courts and council chambers of the world; he also unveils the most sublime mysteries. He commands the Second Legion of Spirits, and has under him *Buer, Gusoyn, and Botis*, etc.

FLEURETY, Lieutenant-General, has the power to perform any labour during the night; he moreover causes hailstorms in any required place.

He controls a very considerable army of Spirits, and has *Bathsin, Pursan, and Eligor*, etc., etc. as his subordinates.

SARGATANES, Brigadier-Major, has the power to make any person invisible, to transport them to any place, to open all locks, to reveal whatsoever is taking place in private houses, to teach all the rogueries of the Shepherds; he commands several Brigades of Spirits, and has *Zoray, Valefar, and Faraii*, etc. fo his immediate inferiors.

NEBIROS, Field-Marshal and Inspector.General has the power to do evil to whomsoever he will; he discovers the Hand of Glory, he reveals all the virtue of Metals, Minerals, Vegetables, and of all Animals both pure and impure. He also possesses the art of predicting things to come, being one of the greates Necromancers in all the Infernal Hierarchies; he goes to and fro everywhere and inspects all the hordes of perdition. His immediate subordinates are *Ayperos, Naberrs, and Glassyalabolas*, etc., etc.

NOTICE.
When you have determined to make a Pact with one of the governing Intellegences which I have just named you must begin on the previous evening by cutting with a new and unused Knife, a Rod of Wild Hazel, which has never borne fruit, and which shall be similar to th Blasting Rod as it has been already described and represented in Book the First.

This must be do precisely at the moment when the sun appears upon our horizon. This being accomplished, arm yourself with the stone called Ematille, and with two blessed Candles, and proceed to select a place for the coming operation, where you will he wholly undisturbed; ye may even make the Pact in some isolated room, or some subterranean part of an old ruinous castle, for the Spirit has the power to transport the Treasure to any required place. This having been arranged, describe a triangle with the stone called Ematille- this is exclusively needed on the first occasion making a Pact. Then set the two blessed Candles in a parallel position on either side of the Triangle of Pacts, inscribing the Holy Name of Jesus below so that no Spirits can injure you after any manner. You may now take up your position in the middle of the triangle, holding the mysterious Rod, together with the grand Conjuration of the Spirit, the Clavicle, the Requisition you mean to make, and the Discharge of the Spirit.

Having exactly fulfilled what things soever have been above described, begin by reciting the following Conjuration with decision and hopefulness.

Grand Conjuration of Spirits with whom it is sought to make a Pact. Taken from the grand Clavicle.

Emperor LUCIFER, Master of all the revolted Spirits, I entreat thee to favour me in the adjuration which I address to thy mighty minister, LUCIFUGE' ROFOCALE, being desirous to make a Pact with him. I beg thee also, o Prince Belzebuth, to protect me in my undertaking! o Count Astarot! be propitious to me and grant that to-night the great LUCIFUGE' may appear to me under a human form, and free from evil smell, and that he may accord me in virtue of the Pact which I propose to enter into all the riches which I need. Oh! grand LUCIFUGE', I pray thee to quit thy dwelling wheresoever it may he, and come hither to speak with me, otherwise will I compel thee by the power of the strong living God, of His beloved Son, and of thee. Obey promptly, or thou shalt lie eternally tormented by the power of the potent words in the grand Clavicle of Solomon, wherewith he was accustomed to compel the rebellious Spirits to receive his Compact. Then straightway appear, or I will persistently torture thee by the virtue of these great words in the Clavicle:

Aglon, Tetragram, vaycheon stimulamaton ezphares retragrammaton olyaram irion esytion existion eryona onera brasym mozm messias soter Emanuel Sabaoth Adonay te adoro, et te invoco. Amen.

You can be certain that before having finished reading the above-mentioned powerful words the spirit will appear and will tell you the following.

Apparition of the Spirit

"Here I am. What would you ask of me? Why do you torment my rest? Answer me!"

—--LUCIFUGE' ROFOCALE.

Request to the Spirit

"I may ask you to make a pact with me so that you make me rich as soon as possible, otherwise I will torment you by the powerful words of the Clavicle.

--KARCIST

Response of the Spirit

I can not grant your request except on the condition that you give yourself to me for the next 20 years so that I can use your body and soul as I see fit.

---LUCIFUGE' ROFOCALE.

Then you will throw him your pact, which must be in your handwritting on a sheet of virgin parchment, which will consist of these few words, with your signature written in your blood. Here is the pact:

"I promise to repay the great Lucifuge in 20 years for all of the treasures that he will give me. On my honor I sign this in good faith."

—Signature in blood

Response of the Spirit

"I can not grant your request."

--LUCIFUGE' ROFOCALE.

48

Seguimi e prendi il tesoro che vado
a mostrarti

" Follow me and take the treasure I will show
you"

SECOND APPEARANCE OF THE SPIRIT

Then, in order to force the spirit to obey you, re-read the great Invocation of the terrible words of the Clavicle, until the spirit appears and tells you the following:

"Why do you torment me more and more? If you leave me in peace, I will give you the nearest treasure on the condition that you consecrate a coin to me all of the Mondays of every month and that you will call me one day every week, from ten o'clock in the evening until 2 two in the morning. Take your pact which I have signed; and if you do not maintain your word you will be mine in 20 years."

--LUCIFUGE ROFOCALE

Response to the Spirit

"I adhere to your demands, on the condition that you enable me to have the nearest treasure and that I can take it with me right away."

--KARCIST

Response of the Spirit

"Follow me and take the treasure that I am going to show you."

--LUCIFUGE ROFOCALE

Then follow the spirit on the path to the treasure that will be indicated (at the triangle) without taking fright and throw the signed pact over the treasure and touching it with the rod take as much of it as you can. Then return inside the triangle, making certain to walk backwards, where you will deposit your treasure in front of yourself, dismissing the spirit as follows:

THE CONJURING AND DISMISSAL OF THE SPIRIT WITH WHOM THE PACT IS MADE

"O great LUCIFUGE, I am satisfied with you at present; I will leave you to peace and permit you to retire to wherever you wish without making any noise or leaving any bad odors. Think then, about your duty regarding my pact; since, if the one instant you shirk your obligation, you can be sure that I will torment you eternally with the great and powerful words of the great Clavicle of the great King Solomon with which he forced all of the rebel spirits to obey him."

PRAYER TO THE OMNIPOTENT IN THANKSGIVING

"Omnipotent God, heavenly father, who created all things for the service and use of man, I humbly thank you, that in your great goodness and that you have permitted that I could make a pact with a spirit that is a rebel of your authority and subdue it to obey me in fulfilling all of my needs. I thank you, o omnipotent God, for the good that you have done me tonight to have shown myself to be worthy to have granted to me, miserable creature, your precious favors and to present, great God, now that I have come to know the force and power of your great promises, when you said: "seek and you shall find", "knock and the door shall be opened" as you have recommended to raise the poor, condescend o great God to inspire me to true sentiment of charity so that I can spread with this Great Work a great portion of the possessions your great divinity permitted that I could receive. Let it be, o great God, that I can enjoy these great riches that I possess, with tranquillity and do not permit any rebel spirit to harm my enjoyment of these precious treasures over which you permit me to own. Inspire in me, o great God, the necessary sentiment to unbind me from the grips of the devil and all maleffcient spirits. I trust, o great God, in the Father, the Son, and the Holy Spirit and in your saintly protrection. Amen."

ORATION TO PROTECT ONESELF FROM EVIL SPIRITS

"O omnipotent Father, o Mother, the most tender of all mothers, oadmirable example of the sentiments, o Son, o flower of all sons, soul, spirit, harmony and number of all orders, preserve us, protect us, guide us and be propitious. Amen."

CITATIO PRAEDICTORUM SPIRITUM

§I.

Ubi quern volueris spiriturn, hujus nornen et officium supra cognosces: imprimis autem ab omni pollutione minimum tres vel quatuor dies mundus esto in prima citatione, sic et spiritus postea obsequentiores erunt; fac et circulum, et voca spiritum, cum multa intentione primum vere anulum in manu contiietur: inde bane resitata benedictionem tuo nomine e socii, si praesto fuerit et effectum tui instituti sortieris, nee detrimentum e spiritibus senties imo tuae animae perditionem.

§II.

In nomine domini nostri Jesus Christi, patris etfilii et spiritus sancti: sancta Trinitas et inseparabilis unitas te invoco, ut sis mihi salus et defensio et protectio corporis et animae meae et omnium rerum mearum. Per virtutem sanctae crucis et per virtutem passionis tuae deprecor te Domine Jesus Christi, per merita beatissimae Mariae Virgin! et matris tuae atque ominus sanctorum tuorum, ut mihi concedas gratiam et potestatem divinam super omnes malignos spiritus, ut quoscumque nominibus invocavero, statim ex omni parte conveniant, et

voluntatem meam perfecte adimpleant qued mihi nihil nocentes, neque timorem
inferentes, sed potens obedientes et ministrantes, tua distincte virtute praecipiente, mandata mea perficiant. Amen.

Sanctus, sanctus, dominus Deus sabaot, qui venturus estjudicare vivos et mortuos: tu qui es primus et novissimus, rex regum et dominum dominantium Joth, Agladabrach, Elabiel. anarchi enatiel amaz in sedomel gayes tol ma elias ischiro atgadatasy mas heli messias per ha tua sancta nomina, et per omnia alia invocare et obsecro te Domine Jesu Christe, per quam nativitatem per baptismum tuum, per passionem et crucem tuam, per ascensionem tuam per adventum Spiritus Sancti paraclite per amaritudinae anime tuae quando exivi de corpore tuo per quinque vulnera tua, per sanguinem et aquam quae exierant de corpore tuo, per virtutem tuam, per sacramentum quod dedisti descipuit tui pridie quam passus fuisti per sanctam Trinitatem, per individuam anitatem, per beatam Mariam, matrem tuam. per Angelos, et arcangelos, per prophetas et patriarchas, et per omnes sancto tuos et per omnia sacramenta quae fiant in honore tuo; adoro et te obsecro, te benedicto tibi, et rogo ut acceptes orationes has et conjurationes et verba oris mei; quibus uti volucro peto Domine Jesu Christe: da mihi virtutem et potestatem tuam super omnes angelos tuos, qui de coelo ejecti sunt ad decipiendum genus humanum; ad attrahendum eos, ad constringendum, ad ligandum eos pariter et solvendum; et ad congregantum eos coram me; quae possunt, faciant et verba mea vocem que meam nullo modo contemnant, sed mihi et dictis meis obediant, et me tineant per humanitatem et misericaridam et gratiam tuam deprecor et peto et ADONAY amay hora videgora mitay hel suranay syota y fiesy, et per omnia uomina tua sancta per omnes sanctos et sanctos tuos, per angelos et archangelos, potestates, dominitiones et virtutes, et per illud nomen per quod Salomo costringebat daemone et conclusit ipso. Eth roceban hrangle goth joih athio venoh aubru et per omnium tua nomina quae scripta sunt in hoc librum et per virtutem sorundem. quatenus me potentem faciat con gregare contringere omnes tuos spiritus de coelo depulsos ut mihi veraciter de omnibus meis interrogatis de quibus quaram responsionem veracem tribuant et omnibus meis mandatis illi satis faciant sine laesione corporis et animae meae, et omnibus ad me pertinentium, per dominum nostrum Jesum Christum filium tuum, qui tecum vivit et tegnat in unitate spiritus sancti Deus, per omnia saecula.

§III.

O pater omnipotens!, o filii sapiens, o spiritus sante corda hominum illustrans' vos tres in personis una vero deltas in substantia qui Adam et Evae in peccatis eorum perpercistis et propter eorum peccata mortem subjesti tu filii turpissima in lignoque sancte crucis sustinuisti. o misericordissime quando ad tuam confugio misericordiam, et supplico modis omnibus quibus possum per haec nomina sancta tui filii scilicet A et a et per omnia alia sua nomina, quatenus concedas mihi virtutem et potestatem tual, ut valeam tuos spiritusqui de coelo ejecti sunt, ante me citare, et ut ipsi mecum loquantur, et mandata mea perficiant statim et fine mora cum eorum voluntate, sine omni laesione corporis animae et honorum meorum. Amen.

§IV.

O summa et eterna virtus altissimi! que te disponente hisjudicio vocatis vaycheon stimulamaton esphares tetagrammaton ilioram rion esytio existioneriona onera brasym moyn messias sodxer, EMMANUEL, SABAOTH, ADONAY, te adoro, te invoco, totius mentis viribus meis. imploro, quaenus perte praesentes orationes et consecrationes consequentur videlicet, et ubicumque maligni spiritus in virtute tuorum dominum sunt vocati, et voluntatem mei exorcisatores diligenter adimpleant fiat, fiat, fiat. Amen.

THE MAGICK SECRET; OR THE ART OF SPEAKING WITH THE DEAD

For this operation it is necessary to attend midnight mass at Christmas and at midnight precisely to have a conversation with the inhabitants of the other world and at the moment that the Priest lifts the Host. bow down and with a frank and severe voice say "Esurgent mortuit et ac me veniut." As soon as you have pronounced these six words it is necessary to go to the cemetery and at the first tomb that meets your eye offer this prayer:

"Infernal powers, you who bring the turbid in the universe, abandon your obscure dwelling and retire to the other side of the River Styx."

Then remain there for a moment of silence.

"If you have your power, he or she that interests me, I supplicate you in the name of the King of Kings to make him appear before me at the hour and moment that I will indicate to you."

After this ceremony, which is indispensable to carry out, take a fistful of earth and spread it as one sows grain in a field, saying in a low voice:

"He who is in dust awake from his tomb and leave his ashes and answer the questions that I pose him in the name of the Father of all men."

Then bend a knee to the ground, turning your eyes to the East and when you see that the doors of the Sun are going to open, arm yourself with the two bones of the dead man that you will put in a cross of Saint Andrew. Then throw them at the first temple or church that offers itself to your eyes.

Having well-executed the aforesaid, set out in a western direction and when you have taken 5,900 steps, lay yourself down to sleep on the ground in an elongated position, holding the palms of your hand against your thighs, and your eyes to the sky towards the Moon and in this position, call he or she whom you wish to see, when you see the specter appear, solicit their presence with the following words

"Ego sum te peto, et videre queo"

After these words, your eyes will be satisfied to see the object that dearest to you and give you the most pleasurable delight.

When you have obtained from the shadow which you have Invoked, that which you believe to be to your satisfaction, send it away in this manner:

"Return to the knqgdom of the elect, I am content with you and your presence."

Then picking yourself up. return to the same tomb where you made the first prayer above which you need to make a cross with the end of your blade which you will be holding in your left hand.

The reader should not neglect any of the prescribed ceremonies otherwise he could incur some risk.

SECRETS OF THE MAGICK ART

Observe that these secrets can not be employed by those who have not done all that is described in Chapters II, III and IV of the first book of this volume.

THE COMPOSITION OF DEATH, OR PHILOSOPHER'S STONE

Take a new earthen pot, put in it a pound of red copper with half a bottle of Nitric Acid. Boil it for half an hour. Afterwards add three ounces ofverdegris (Copper Carbonate), and boil for one hour. Then add two and a half ounces of arsenic, and boil one hour. Add three ounces of oak bark, well pulverized, and let it boil a half hour, add a 64 fluid ounces of rose water boil twelve minutes, then add three ounces of lampblack, and let it boil until the composition is good. To see whether it is cooked enough, dip a nail in it; if it adheres, remove it. It will produce a pound and a half of good gold. If it does not adhere, it is proof that it has not cooked enough; the liquor can serve four times.

TO MAKE THE DIVINING ROD AND MAKE IT WORK

At the moment the sun appears on the horizon, take your left hand a virgin branch from the wild hazel tree, and cut it in three strokes while saying:

"I collect you in the name of ELOHIM, MITRATHON. ADONAY and SEMIPHORAS, so that you have the virtue of the rod of Moses and Jacob, to discover all that I will want to know."

To make it work, hold it tightly in your hands by the two ends which make the fork, and say:

"I command you in the name of ELOHIM, MITRATHON, ADONAY and SEMIPHORAS to reveal to me, etc."

TO ENCHANT FIREARMS

Say: "God has a share in it and the devil has the exit', and when you fire, say the following while crossing your left leg over your right: 'non tradas Dominum nostrum Jesum Christum. Mathon. Amen."

TO WIN ANY TIME ONE PLAYS THE LOTTERY

Lying down, recite three times the following prayer, after what to you will put it under your pillow, written on virgin parchment, on which you will have a mass of the Holy Spirit said, and during sleep the genius of your planet will come and tell you the hour that you must get your ticket.

"Domine Jesu Christe, qui dixisti ego sum via, veritas et vita, ecce enim veritatem dilexisti, incerta et occulta sapientise fuse manifestasti mihi, adhuc quse reveles in hac node sicut ita revelatum fuit parvulis solis, incognita et ventura unaque alia me doceas, ut possim omnia cognoscere, si et si sit; ita monstra mihi montem ornatum omni nivo bono, pulchrum et gratum pomarium, aut quandam rem gratam, sin autem ministra mihi ignem ardentem, vel aquarum currentem vel aliam quamcumque rem quse Domino placeat, et vel Angeli ARIEL, Rubiel et Barachiel sitis mihi multum amatores et factores ad opus istud obtinendum quod cupio scire, vide re cognoscere et prsevidere per ilium Deum qui venturus est judicare vivos et mortuos, et sseculum per ignem. Amen."

Say three "Our Father" 's and three "Hail Mary" 's for the souls left in purgatory.

TO SPEAK WITH THE SPIRITS ON THE EVE OF ST. JOHN THE BAPTIST

From eleven at night until Midnight go stand by a fern, and say: "I ask of God that the spirits with which I wish to speak will appear at precisely midnight"; and at three-quarters repeat nine times these five words: Bar. Kirabar, Alii, Alia Tetragrammaton.

TO BE INSENSIBLE TO TORTURE

Write these lines on a small piece of paper, which you will then swallow.

Dismas et gestas damnatur potestas.
Disma et gestas damnatur.
Ad astra levatur.

When you will have to be tortured say: "This rope is so soothing to the my limbs, like the Holy Virgin's milk to Our Lord."

TO COMPEL ONE DANCE COMPLETELY NAKED

On Eve of St. John the Baptist, gather at midnight, three walnut leaves, three sweet marjoram plants, three myrtle plants, and three vervain plants. Dry it all in the shade, and make it into a powder. When you want to make use of the powder, Throw some like a small pinch of tobacco into the air of the room where there are the people whom you wish to enjoy.

TO MAKE ONESELF INVISIBLE

Take a black cat, and a new pot, a mirror, a lighter, coal and tinder.

Gather water from a fountain at the strike of midnight.

After you light your fire, and put the cat in the pot. Hold the cover with your left hand without moving nor looking behind you, no matter what noises you may hear.

After having made it boil 24 hours, putthe boiled cat on a new dish. Take the meat and throw it over your left shoulder, saying these words: "accipe quod tibi do, et nihil amplius."

Then put the bones one by one under the teeth on the left side, while looking at yourself in the mirror; and if they are do not work, throw them away, repeating the same words each time until you find the right bone; and as soon you cannot see yourselve any more in the mirror, withdraw, moving backwards, while saying:

"Pater, in manus tuas commendo spiritum meum."

This is bone you must keep.

TO RENDER ONESELF FAVORABLE TO JUDGES

Upon seeing the Judge, say these words: "Phalay. Phalay, Phalay; preside in my favor, let your power shine. Make me satisfied." To be Impervios to White Arms

With the head of a needle, write these words on your arm: Ales †
Dales † Tolas †. Then put the needle in the middle cross, from which no blood will flow.

TO MAKE THE GARTER OF TWENTY MILES PER HOUR

Buy a young wolf under one year old, and cut its throat with a new knife, in the hour of Mars, pronouncing these words: Adhumatis cados ambulavit in fortitudine cibi ilius; then cut his skin into broad garters of an inch, and write there upon the same words that you said while slaughtering it. Write the first letter with your blood, the second with that of the wolf, and continue in the same way until the end of the sentence.

After it is written and dries, it is necessary to cover it by wrapping the garter in white cloth, and to attach two purple ribbons to the two ends, so to tie the garters to the knee braces; Make sure that no woman or girl sees the garters; also remove the garters before crossing a river, Less it loses it's power.

FORMULA FOR A PLASTER TO TRAVEL TEN MILES PER HOUR

Take two ounces of human fat, one ounce of oil of stag, one ounce of oil of bay-tree, one ounce of fat of stag, one ounce of natural mummy, a half-cup of spirit of wine, and seven vervain leaves. Boil the whole in a new pot, until half- reduction, then form a plaster of it on a fresh wolf skin. When you wear it on the spleen, you go like the wind.

To not fall when you are done, take three drops of blood in a glass of white wine and soak your feet in the wine.

COMPOSITION OF THE INK FOR WRITING PACTS

The pacts should not be written with ordinary ink. It must be changed each time that there is occasion to write a pact, that is to say, whenever the appellation of a spirit is made. Place river-water in a new, water-proof earthenware pot, together with the powder described below. Take sprigs of fern gathered on the Eve of St. John and vine twigs cut in the full moon of March. Kindle this wood by means of virgin paper, and when the water boils the ink will be made. It must be changed each time that there is occasion to write, that is to say, whensoever the appellation of a spirit is undertaken.

10 oz. Of Gall nuts, 3 oz. Of Roman Vitriol or Green Copperas, 3 oz. Of Rock Alum or dried Gum Arabic. Make a fine powder, and when you would compose the ink, use as described above.

SOLOMON'S MIRROR

How to Make Solomon's Mirror
† in nomine domini. amen. †

The manner upon which the Cabbalist Scholars relied to make the Mirror of Solomon, David's son, who had the gift of wisdom and the occult science; this mirror is made in forty-eight days, starting from the New Moon until the following Full one. You will see (in this mirror) all of the hidden things that you desire in the name of our Lord.

First, abstain from any carnal action or thought for the entire aforementioned time and meanwhile do many pious and compassionate deeds.

Take a shiny and well cleaned plate of steel and write in the four corners these precise words in the blood of a White Dove: JEHOVA, ELOHIM, MITRATHON, ADONAY. Then put the steel plate in a piece of new white cloth and when you observe the New Moon one hour after the sun has set go to the window and gazing at the sky and the moon say with devotion:

"O rex eternae Deus! Creator ineffabilis, qui cuncta as hominis sanitatem meagratio, et occulto judicio creasti respice me (N.N.), indignissimum servum tuum, et ad intentionem meam, et mittere mihi dignare angelum Anael, in speculum istud, qui mandet, et inspiret etjubeat cum sociis suis, et subditis nostris ut in nominee tuo qui fuisti, es et eris potens, etjus, jud, judicent mihi quecumque ab ill is exposcam."

Take some ashes made from Laurel wood and add some perfume into it in three shots saying:

"In hoc, per hoc, et cum hoc, quod effundo ante conspectum tuum, Deus meus, trinus et unus benedictus et per excelsus qui vides super Cherubin et Seraphin et venturus estjudicare seculum per ignem."

Recite this prayer three times, blow on the mirror and then call out this invocation: "Veni Anael, et tibi complaceat esse persocios tuos mecum, in nomine paths potentissimi, in nomine filio sapientissimo, in nomine spiritus amabilissimi. Veni Anael, in nomini terribilis JEHOVA; veni Anael in virtute immortalis Eliom; veni Anael in brachio omnipotentis Mitraton; veni Anael in potentia sacratissimi ADONAY; veni ad me (N.N.) in ispeculo isto, etjubeat subditis tuis ut cum amore gaudio et pace ostendat mihi occulta in oculis meis. Amen."

This said, raise your eyes to the sky and say:

"Domini Deus omnipotens, cujus nutu omnia moventur, exaudi deprecationem meum et desiderium meum tibi complaceat, respice domini speculum istud, et benedice illi ut Anael, unus ex subditis fuisse sistat in illo cum sociis et satisfaciat mihi famulo tuo (N.N.), cui vivis et regnas benedictus et excelsus, in saecula saeculorum. Amen."

After the aforementioned prayer, cross yourself and the mirror, and this you will do everyday for as long as it takes to make the mirror. In the end, the angel Anael will appear in the guise of a most handsome young man will greet you and command his companions to obey you. Be aware that 48 days are not always necessary to obtain what you intend; often he appears after 14 days, that depends on the intention and devotion of the Operator.

So when the spirit appears to you, as him everything that you wish and request that he appear to you whenever you call him to satisfy your requests. Then you will see everything you wish to see

without reciting the preceding oration; but having anointed him
with scent (the scent of Anael is Saffron) say the following:

ORATION

"Veni Anael, veni tibi complaceat esse persocios tuos mecum, in nomini mecum, in nomini Pains potentissimi, in nomini Filii sapientissimi, in nomine Spiritus Sancti amabilissimi; veni Anael, in virtutis immortal is ELOHIM; veni Anael, in brachio omnipotentis Mitraton; veni Anael, in potentia sacratissimi ADONAY; veni ad me (N.N.) in speculo isto, etjubeas subditis tuis, ut cum amore, gaudio et
pace ostendam mihi occulta inoculis meis. Amen, Amen."

After you have recited this oration he will appear to you and satisfy all ofyour desires.

METHOD OF TAKING LEAVE OF THE ANGEL ANAEL

"Gratias tibi ago Anael quod venisti, et petition! mese satisfecisti, ibi in pace et placeat tibi redire quando to vocavero."

Cross yourself and the mirror.

TABLE OF AUSPICIOUS AND INAUSPICIOUS DAYS

Auspicious Days	Month	Inauspicious Days
3,10, 27 and 31	January	13 and 23
7, 8 and 18	February	2,10,17 and 22
3, 9,12,14 and 16	March	13,19, 23 and 28
5 and 17	April	18, 20, 29 and 30
1,2, 4, 6, 9 and 14	May	10,17 and 20
3, 5, 7, 9, 12 and 23	June	4 and 20
2, 6,10, 23 and 30	July	5,13 and 27
5, 7,10,14 and 29	August	2,13, 27 and 31
6,10,13,18 and 30	September	13,16,18 and 19
13,16, 25 and 31	October	3, 9 and 27
1,13, 23 and 30	November	6 and 25
10, 20 and 29	December	15, 26 and 31

OBSERVATION

Many wise men believe this table was dictated to Abraham by an angel and that it determined his actions: he neither sowed nor transplanted except on   auspicipus days and for this reason everything went marvelously for him. If your ploughmen did likewise their yield would certainly increase.

THE SECRET OF THE BLACK HEN

The famous secret of the Black Hen, a secret without which one can not count on the success of any cabala, was lost for a long time: after much investigation we have succeeded in finding it and the tests which we have carried out, to assure ourselves that it was positively that which we sought, exactly matched our expectations. Therefore we are completely satified. It is to share our happiness with all those who have the courage to imitate us that we have transcribed it.

Take a Black Hen that has never been laid eggs and that has never been approached by a rooster and in taking her make certain that she does not cry out so that you will have to do this at eleven at night, when she is sleeping. Take her neck and close her throat so that she can not scream.

Then go where two streets form a cross and at midnight precisely make a circle with a Cyprus branch, go into the middle of the circle and cut the hen's body into two parts uttering the following words three times: ELOHIM, ESSAIM, search and then turn your gaze toward the East, kneel and recite the prayer:

PRAYER TO THE OMNIPOTENT IN THANKSGIVING

"Omnipotent God, heavenly father, who created all things for the service and use of man, I humbly thank you, that in your great goodness and that you have permitted that I could make a pact with a spirit that is a rebel of your authority and subdue it to obey me in fulfilling all of my needs. I thank you, O omnipotent God, for the good that you have done me tonight to have shown myself to be worthy to have granted to me, miserable creature, your precious favors and to present, great God, now that I have come to know the force and power of your great promises, when you said: "seek and you shall find", "knock and the door shall be opened" as you have recommended to raise the poor, condescend o great God to inspire me to true sentiment of charity so that I can spread with this Great Work a great portion of the possessions your great divinity permitted that I could receive. Let it be, O great God, that I can enjoy these great riches that I possess, with tranquillity and do not permit any rebel spirit to harm my enjoyment of these precious treasures over which you permit me to own. Inspire in me, O great God, the necessary sentiment to unbind me from the grips of the devil and all maleffcient spirits. I trust, O great God, in the Father, the Son, and the Holy Spirit and in your saintly protrection. Amen."

ORATION TO PROTECT ONESELF FROM EVIL SPIRITS

"O omnipotent Father, o Mother, the most tender of all mothers, O admirable example of the sentiments, O Son, O flower of all sons, soul, spirit, harmony and number of all orders, preserve us, protect us, guide us and be propitious. Amen."

GREAT INVOCATION TO SUMMON THE SPIRIT WITH WHOM ONE WISHES TO THE PACT EXCERPTED FROM THE GREAT CLAVICLE

"Emperor LUCIFER, master of all the rebel spirits, I ask you to be favorable in my summons of your Great Minister LUCIFUGE ROFOCALE, since I wish to make a pact with him. I also request that you, Prince BELZEBUTH, protect me in my undertaking; O Come ASTAROTH BE propitious and ensure that the great LUCIFUGE appears to me tonight in human guise and without emitting foul odors and he grant me as per the pact that I will present to him, all of the riches which I require. O great LUCIFUGE, I request that you abandon your dwelling, in whatever part of the world it should be, to come and speak with me. Otherwise, I will force you by the power of the great living God and his dear Son and the Holy Spirit: obey now, or I will eternally torment you by the authority of the powerful words of Solomon's great Clavicle of which he made use to oblige the rebel Spirits to receive his pact; therefore, appear as quickly as possible or I will continually torment you by the authority of the powerful words of the Clavicle: Aglon, Tetragram, vaychen stimulamaton ezphares Tetragrammaton,olyaram irion esytion existion eryona onera orasim mozm messias soter EmanuelSabaoth ADONAY, te adoro et te invoco. Amen."

At that moment the foul spirit will appear, dressed in a scarlet outfit with braids, a yellow shirt, green pants, his head resembles that of a dog, but he has the ears of an ass, with two horns, legs and feet like a heifer. He will ask you your demands; you give them as you think best since he will not be able to disobey you and he can make you one of the richest and therefore happiest of men.

Before you do what has been explained you need to make your devotions. Say your prayers and be above reproach; this is so essential that in doing the opposite you could end up at the spirits command, instead of him being at yours.

OTHER MAGICK SECRETS

TO PREVENT A WOMAN FROM CONCEIVING

To prevent a woman, with whom you are having relations, from having children, take a sponge the size of a nutmeg, and soak it with pure milk mixed with a little fine oil. Put it in her left hand and walk away from her and every time you do this you will be sure to gave good results.

TO FIND OUT WHETHER A WOMAN CAN HAVE CHILDREN

Take the fat of a dear, melt it in hot water; the woman should drink it on an empty stomach and afterwards take a hot bath. If this gives her pain in her stomach, then she will have children, otherwise not.

TO MAKE THREE YOUNG LADIES, OR RATHER THREE SPIRITS COME INTO YOUR ROOM AFTER DINNER

PREPARATION

Eat neither meat nor fatty foods for three days; on the fourth day clean your room as soon as you have arisen from bed, fast for the entire day and ensure that no one enters the room all day and that there is nothing hung on the walls, neither clothes, nor hats, nor bird cages, nor curtains on the windows or on the bed and above all, put freshly washed white linens on the bed.

CEREMONY

After dinner, go secretly to the room that you have prepared, light a good fire, put a clean white cloth on the table and three chairs around the table and three loaves of bread and three glasses of clear, fresh water at each place. Then put a recliner or chair beside your bed and get into bed.

Upon entering the room the three persons will seat themselves beside the fire and taking refreshment and thank he or she who has received them, since, if he is a man who makes the ceremony three ladies will come, and if it is a woman, three men will come. The three spirits will choose by lots among themselves to determine who will remain seated in the chair beside your bed to converse with you until midnight.

At midnight she will leave with her companions without you having to ask her to leave, as for the other two, they will remain by the fire while the other converses with you beside your bed and you will to ask her about any art or science that you desire and she will immediately answer your questions, you can ask her the location of the nearest hidden treasure and she will reveal to you the most opportune time and place to recover it. She will also be there accompanied by her two companions to protect you from any infernal spirit who could be in possession of the treasure. When she leaves, she will give you a ring which will make you lucky in any game when you wear it and if you place it on a young maid's finger you can make her your wife.

Note: Leave the window open so that they may enter and you can repeat this operation and make them come as many times as you wish. You should repeat the following prayer after each conjuration:

"O summa et eterna virtus altissimi! que te disponente his judicio vocatis vaycheon stimulamaton esphares tetagrammaton ilioram rion esytio existioneriona onera brasym moyn messias sodxer, EMMANUEL, SABAOTH, ADONAY, te adoro, te invoco, totius mentis viribus meis, imploro, quaenus perte praesentes orationes et consecrationes consequentur videlicet, et ubicumque maligni spiritus in virtute tuorum dominum sunt vocati, et voluntatem mei exorcisatores diligenter adimpleant fiat, fiat, fiat. Amen."

TO BE LUCKY IN EVERY ENTERPRISE

Take a green frog, cut off its head and his four feet. Then on a Friday with a full Moon put them in an elder tree and keep them there for twenty-one days, removing them on the twenty-first dat precisely at midnight.

Then expose the parts of the frog to the light of the Moon for three nights. Afterwards, dry the frog parts in a new earthernware pot that has never been used. Take the dried frog parts, and grind to a powder. Mix the powder in equal measure with earth taken from a cemetery, if possible from the grave of someone in your family.

Carry the powder mixture with you, it will help you succeed in any undertaking.

(

TO MAKE A WOMAN DISCLOSE HER SECRETS

Take the heart of a pigeon and the head of a frog. Dry them as above, and reduce them to fine powder. Put the powder into a little purse, and add moss for frangrance.

Put the purse under the woman's ear while she is sleeping, fifteen minutes later, she will unveil all of her secrets. Make certain to remove the purse a few minutes after she has stopped speaking otherwise she could fall into delirium.

TO SEE AND DO THE SUPERNATURAL

Put a gold studded plate under your tongue, it should be half the size of your thumb. Under your feet put the border of a mortuary sheet or linen and hold a quince tree branch in your hand. Abstain from having sexual relations for thirty-five days, for thirty-five is the number that puts you under the protection of favorable constellations and sorcery and with this secret one can do prodigious deeds, as did Mousu with this secret did supernatural things.

TO MAKE EVERYTHING IN AN APARTMENT APPEAR BLACK

Soak the wick of the lamp used to light the apartment in well beaten sea foam, adding to the lamp oil some sulfur and Litharge in equal parts, and all those who enter the room will appear drunk and delirious.

GLUE TO ATTACH CRYSTALS

Take some wine spirits and whitest and clearest Gum Arabic. Liquefy the Gum Arabic with the spirits. Heat up the two broken pieces in the fire, then with a little brush apply the glue to the two pieces. Attach the two pieces, and hold together until they have cooled.

GLUE TO REPAIR PORCELAIN VASES

Take two fresh egg whites, mix them together, add a little quicklime. Put a little of this mixture on the broken pieces, hold them together for two or three minutes.

Then boil them with milk and the cracks will become invisible.

THE SECRETS OF LOVE OF RECIPROCAL LOVE BETWEEN A MAN AND A WOMAN

There is nothing more natural to man than loving and being loved.

Without invoking Venus or Cupid, who are the dominant divinities regarding this noble passion of man, every day produces material substances that are favorable to success in love.

One often finds on the forehead of a newborn foal, a little piece of flesh that has marvelous virtue in love. Dry it in a new pot. and wear it, especially on Fridays, since this is the day dedicated to Venus, Goddess of Love.

ANOTHER LOVE SECRET

Take a gold ring that is studded with a small diamond that has not been worn by anyone. Wrap it in a piece of green fabric and for nine days and nine nights wear it against your skin over your heart. On the ninth day, before the Sun rises, engrave the following word inside the ring: Scheva, with a new scribe or engraver.

Find a way to have three hairs of the person who you want to love you, unite them with three of your own hairs, while saying:

"Body, that you could love me, that your desires could be as passionate as mine, by Scheva's most potent virtue."

Tie the hairs in a love snare knot around the ring. Wrap the ring in a piece of silk, and wear it against your skin over your heart for another six days.

On the seventh day. Fast. On an empty stomach, unwrap the ring and give it to the person you desire to love you.

If your ring is accepted then you can be certain to be loved by that person. If the ring is refused, rest assured that the heart of that person belongs to another and in that case, you should seek your fortune elsewhere.

OTHER SECRETS THAT ACHIEVE THE SAME EFFECT

Here is the secret that the wise Cabbalists have called "Apple of Love" which is prepared as follows:

Go pick an apple from a tree on a Friday morning before sunrise. Writeyour name with your blood on a piece of paper and also write the name of the person whom you wish to love you. On another sheet of paper, write the name Scheva, also in your own blood.

Find a means of procuring three strands of that person's hair, which you will unite with three of yours. Cut the apple in half, and remove the seeds. In the place of the seeds, place the pieces of paper. Take the apple and tie it back together, with the united hairs, using a green myrtle twig to twist together the two halves of the apple like a tourniquet.

Dry well in the oven, and wrap them in bay and myrtle leaves. Have a well trusted person put the apple under the young woman's pillow without her noticing. In a few days you will notice the appearance of her love.

Fin

CPSIA information can be obtained at www.ICGtesting.com
Printed in the USA
LVOW04s0325030115

421320LV00030B/2798/P